FUNDAMENTALS OF ESSAY WRITING: AN ORIENTATION MANUAL

FUNDAMENTALS OF ESSAY WRITING: AN ORIENTATION MANUAL

Questions, Answers, And Examples Concerning Effective Essay Writing

by Erskine Peters, Ph.D.

2nd Revised Edition

MAJOR POINTS ON
— Getting Started
— Brainstorming
— Organizing
— Punctuation
— Documentation
— Overcoming Writer's Block
— Writing Book Reviews

Library of Congress Cataloging-in-Publication Data

Peters, Erskine.
    Fundamentals of essay writing.

    1. English language -- Rhetoric.   2. Essay
I. Title.
PE1471.P47   1987   808'.042   86-28006
ISBN 0-916147-05-3

Dedicated to
my students

© 1983 by Erskine Peters

Revised Edition of
Essay Writing: An Orientation Manual
© 1987 by Erskine Peters

2nd Edition With Additions
© 1990 by Erskine Peters

For information regarding the
use of this book contact:

Regent Press
6020-A Adeline Street
Oakland, CA 94608

Manufactured in the United states of America

PREFACE

Everyone can improve his or her writing ability. Effective essay writing is in most cases an acquired skill. It is not a subject so much as it is a process and skill based on techniques. The techniques of the process can be incorporated into one's consciousness and drawn upon according to one's particular needs and at one's convenience. The questions, answers, and examples presented here are intended to aid in the acquisition of these skills.

This book has been prepared to help identify, clarify, and address the particular writing needs and problems confronting all essay writers from time to time. This is a book designed to help orient and re-orient the writer toward what he or she should be preoccupied with whenever undertaking projects in essay writing.

The only way for this book to be of help, of course, is

that it be used—both as a friend and a guide for understanding how to proceed in originating, developing, organizing, and completing the effective essay. The book is also designed to serve as a clarification reference, aiding students in understanding instructors' comments and in undertaking revisions.

It is hoped that the book, if introduced to students at the beginning of a course, will curtail many problems growing out of students' innocence of basic principles, procedures, and definitions. Hopefully, the brevity of the book will encourage instructors and students to make use of its offerings before plunging into writing. —E. P.

ACKNOWLEDGEMENTS

The first printing of this book was made possible through a grant from the Council on Educational Development at the University of California at Berkeley. I am very grateful.

Grateful acknowledgement is made to the James Weldon Johnson Collection curators at Yale University's Beinecke Library for permission to reprint the Frederick Douglass materials.

Special thanks to Elfreda Chatman for lots of energy given to reading the first drafts. Thanks to Elmirie Robinson, Sydné Mahone and Renée Smith for the typing and to Harry Elam, Robert Hollis, and Troy Thibodeaux for assistance with the proof-reading.

CONTENTS

PREFACE i

I

WHAT ARE THE FUNDAMENTAL STEPS
OF ESSAY WRITING? 9

II

WHAT IS A GOOD WRITER? 11

WHAT DO GOOD WRITERS DO WITH LANGUAGE? .. 11

WHAT IS THE SPECIAL IDENTITY OF A WRITER? .. 12

iii

HOW CAN YOU THINK OF YOURSELF
AS A WRITER? 12

HOW IS SELF-CONCEPT RELATED
TO WRITING ABILITY? 12

BY WHAT CRITERIA ARE MOST
WRITERS JUDGED? 13

HOW CAN YOU ANTICIPATE AND FREE YOURSELF
FROM A READER'S CRITICISM? 13

HOW DOES THE WRITER PASS
THE READER'S TEST? 14

HOW SHOULD YOU DISCIPLINE YOUR MIND
AS A WRITER? 15

WHAT IS THE RELATIONSHIP BETWEEN GOOD
WRITING AND GOOD THINKING? 15

WHAT'S WRONG WITH SLANG? 16

HOW CAN YOUR READING TECHNIQUES
HELP YOUR WRITING? 17

WHAT DOES IT MEAN TO ANALYZE, AND
WHAT DOES IT MEAN TO INTERPRET? 17

WHAT IS A GOOD WAY TO STRENGTHEN
THE CLARITY OF YOUR WRITING? 17

WHAT IS FLUENCY? 18

HOW CAN YOU ACHIEVE FLUENCY? 18

WHAT ARE THE BASIC REQUIREMENTS FOR
EFFECTIVE PERFORMANCE IN WRITING? 19

WHAT ARE THE BEST WAYS FOR GETTING
STARTED ON A WRITING PROJECT? 19

HOW CAN YOU BEST JUDGE YOUR READINESS
TO BEGIN A WRITING PROJECT? 20

WHAT IS NOTE-TAKING, AND WHAT
ARE ITS BENEFITS? 20

WHAT IS AN OUTLINE, AND WHAT ARE
ITS BENEFITS? 20

WHAT IS AN INTRODUCTION, AND
WHY DO YOU NEED ONE? 21

WHAT ARE OTHER BENEFITS OF A
GOOD INTRODUCTION? 21

WHAT IS RE-WRITING? 22

HOW CAN YOU SURMOUNT SPECIFIC
PROBLEMS LIKE WRITER'S BLOCK? 22

WHAT AMOUNT OF TIME DOES IT
TAKE TO WRITE? 23

WHAT IS THE BEST PROCEDURE TO USE
WHEN YOU ARE SHORT OF TIME? 23

III
ESSENTIAL TERMINOLOGY AND ELEMENTS IN ESSAY WRITING

WHAT IS DICTION? 24

WHAT IS SYNTAX? 24

WHAT IS PUNCTUATION? 24

WHAT IS GRAMMAR? 24

WHAT IS A SENTENCE? 25

WHAT IS A PARAGRAPH? 25

WHAT IS AN ESSAY? 25

WHAT ARE THE BROADEST CATEGORIES
OF ESSAYS? 26

WHAT ARE THE BASIC MODES OR FORMS OF
DISCOURSE IN WHICH ESSAYS ARE WRITTEN? 26

WHAT ARE THE BENEFITS OF USING THE
COMPARISON/CONTRAST TECHNIQUES
WHEN WORKING WITH THE FOUR
MODES OF DISCOURSE? 29

IV
PUNCTUATION AND OTHER
BASIC RULES OF MECHANICS

WHAT ARE RULES AND EXAMPLES FOR
PUNCTUATING WITH THE COMMA? 31

WHAT ARE RULES AND EXAMPLES FOR
PUNCTUATING WITH THE SEMI-COLON? 34

WHAT ARE OTHER BASIC RULES
OF MECHANICS? 36

V
DOCUMENTATION OF SOURCES:
REFERENCE CITATIONS
(Footnotes, Endnotes, and Bibliographies)

REFERENCE CITATIONS 37

STYLES OF DOCUMENTATION 39

TYPES OF CITATIONS 40

POINTS TO CONSIDER 42

SAMPLE A 44

SAMPLE B 47

VI
WRITING THE BOOK REVIEW ESSAY

WHAT IS A BOOK REVIEW 51

PROCEDURES AND POINTS TO CONSIDER 53

VII

CONCLUSION 57

APPENDIX:
FREDERICK DOUGLASS' CORRESPONDENCE WITH
H. C. WRIGHT CONCERNING HIS MANUMISSION
PAPERS AS AN EXAMPLE OF ARGUMENTATIVE
WRITING EMPLOYING OTHER MODES
OF DISCOURSE 59

INDEX 71

I
WHAT ARE THE FUNDAMENTAL STEPS OF ESSAY WRITING?

- Take on a subject.

- Become involved with the subject:
  - Think about it.
  - Read about it.
  - Talk about it.

- Collect your thoughts on paper about it.

- Formulate your conclusions about it.

- Write about it.

- Re-write about it.

II

WHAT IS A GOOD WRITER?

Good writers are persuasive writers. Their words carry weight and credibility. Good writers convey a sense of authority over the words they use as well as over the subject being treated. Often your problem with writing may not be in not knowing the grammar or the language, but in the way you use the language—or really do not use it.

WHAT DO GOOD WRITERS DO WITH LANGUAGE?

With sincere commitment to their task, good writers put the language to work in order to make it convey their feelings and thoughts. If you are reluctant to use the language, you will not achieve much through it. Language is a birthright. It was created and can be recreated by you for the expression of your particular being. The language is yours to the extent that you operate it and understand the nature of its operation. The subject matter is yours to the extent that you confront it, delve into it and speak about it with discernment and authority. Unless you become actively engaged in writing, you probably will not accomplish very much. You may assemble some information, but your control over it may not be very convincing.

WHAT IS THE SPECIAL IDENTITY OF A WRITER?

Every writer is an ambassador of the language, holding rank based upon how well he or she presents the subject at hand and uses the language as the subject's vehicle. It is by this standard that we generally evaluate a writer. You also evaluate writers all the time, whether reading newspaper articles, books, or journals. If you wish to improve your writing, you too must be conscious of being an ambassador of the language.

HOW CAN YOU THINK OF YOURSELF AS A WRITER?

As one engaged with writing as a growth process, you want to locate or create within your own mind a fertile point upon which you can focus your involvement. Therefore, you should learn to evaluate the various aspects of your writing ability. How good are you in writing introductions? How good are you in stating points clearly? How good are you at deriving interpretations? Develop your own yard stick. One of the best ways to do this is by continuously reading good writers and by measuring yourself against them, especially those writers you most admire.

HOW IS SELF-CONCEPT RELATED TO WRITING ABILITY?

Learning to write effectively can be undertaken as an excercise for inner growth. If you are too skeptical about the worth of your own native intelligence, you may allow this skepticism to interfere with the development or unleashing of your skills as a writer. Too much skepticism can thwart the self-confidence you may need in order to be engaging and exploratory in the subject you are handling.

A good writer needs to cultivate self-confidence. This does not mean that you have license to be presumptuous, however. The presumptuous writer is at the other extreme of the overly skeptical one. He is often superficial, takes too much for granted, slights important meanings, and overlooks the greater potential of language. Be rigorous with yourself, your own emotive and intellectual processes.

BY WHAT CRITERIA ARE MOST WRITERS JUDGED?

The one question common to every reader is: how much can I trust the writer? As a writer, your overall qualitative aims should be thoroughness and precision in your presentation. Thoroughness is what your reader will be expecting. Constant practice of precision will help to keep your subject well-focused.

HOW CAN YOU ANTICIPATE AND FREE YOURSELF FROM A READER'S CRITICISM?

If you can state your point of view, you should also be able to defend it. If you are prepared to offer defense, you must also have a plan. Certainly, too, if there is a plan, there are stages to the plan. This is what the body of your essay is all about. Thus, you must be committed to working out the essay's development. Organize your thoughts and materials so that the treatment of one aspect of the subject will progress smoothly to a discussion of the next aspect. If you do not have a good point of focus or plan of organization, you are penalizing yourself from the outset. Your thoughts and feelings will not be most effectively communicated. You cannot blame the reader for not understanding what you do not write.

If all that you present in the body of your essay is given as direct and substantive support, proof and demonstration of your thesis, and if it is presented via a good plan, your essay should be coherent. You would not only have discussed the different parts, but you would have related them to each other. It is by bringing out the relationships between the parts and by arranging the parts so that they connect smoothly that the total body of the essay holds together.

HOW DOES THE WRITER PASS THE READER'S TEST?

Plan to cover a specified and restricted area. Know whether you are planning to write a book or an essay. Even if you are writing a book you cannot cover everything. When you know your focus, you can restrict your thesis or statement of purpose. A well restricted title is a good start to making an even better thesis statement. The restricted and clear thesis statement is crucial for anchoring your thoughts. The well restricted and clear thesis statement sets boundaries for your reader and yourself.

Whenever possible, it is best to write about subjects in which you have some interest. Since choosing your own subject is not always possible, you can learn to cultivate the skill of developing interest in areas which are either unfamiliar or somewhat unstimulating to you. What you write about the subject will be your intellectual and, perhaps, emotional response to your investigation. Under any circumstances, you will need to have a response if you are to have something to write about. If you have examined your subject at all, you must have something to say about it.

Always maintain rigorous self-scrutiny as you examine your subject. Faulty thoughts and responses will only weaken your attempts in writing.

HOW SHOULD YOU DISCIPLINE YOUR MIND AS A WRITER?

Be discriminating and rigorous in your thinking. Be selective but thorough with the materials you use to support your points. The reader who knows little or nothing about your topic will want to see how well you can inform and stimulate him. The reader who knows something about your topic will be interested to see how well you know it and whether you can add something to what he already knows. Set high standards for yourself, qualifying the materials you use. As a result, what you have to say will be all the more convincing. Push yourself to reveal more of the dimensions of your material than the surface aspects.

You should study the support materials you have accumulated to see how to make the best use of them. Being selective with the materials you employ will demonstrate your familiarity with your subject and the range and depth of your intellect. Discriminate writing and thorough writing work hand-in-hand to enhance your authority over your subject.

WHAT IS THE RELATIONSHIP BETWEEN GOOD WRITING AND GOOD THINKING?

Good thinking and good writing are inseparable. When we think about what we are saying and how it is being said, we necessarily become concerned with organization, logic, punctuation, etc. There may be times when your thoughts are confusing even to you as the creator of the thoughts. The advantage to working with them on paper, however, is that you are giving them a more objective existence. This means you can use your eyes, hands, and mind to work out their clarity.

Write with consciousness of the original context from which you are drawing your material. Be faithful to that context and be critical of it, too, if necessary. You do not have to repeat all the details of the context but your writing with a sense of the context will enrich the new thoughts you are trying to formulate and weave together.

Our naive and simplistic writing styles and choppy sentences are often caused by not thinking deeply about the subject matter. Consequently, we fall into citing too many details and into being too matter-of-fact. We merely end up stating points without really connecting them as thoughts or without developing their meanings as ideas. It is a different matter, however, if we have been asked simply to cite data for an uninterpretative report. In that case, we should be matter-of-fact.

WHAT'S WRONG WITH SLANG?

There's nothing wrong with slang used in its proper element and context. It takes a powerful writer, however, to make very effective use of slang words and phrases in written communication. This is because slang expressions are often rather nebulous—and generally require extra-literary and oral communication features such as intonation, pitch, and physical gesture to render precise and definite meaning.

The frequent user of slang generally suffers from an underused or inadequately developed vocabulary, which, though, can be improved upon.

HOW CAN YOUR READING TECHNIQUES HELP YOUR WRITING?

In order to become a more effective writer, you can also practice reading for writing skills. You can read to learn the writing process by seeing how celebrated, good writers organize what they have to say, building upon words, phrases, sentences and paragraphs to make their meanings clear.

WHAT DOES IT MEAN TO ANALYZE, AND WHAT DOES IT MEAN TO INTERPRET?

Good discussion is built on analysis and interpretation of the data being considered. In order to analyze, select a concept, idea, point of view, theme, image, character, or some aspect of what is pertinent to your subject, and examine it from different angles. Discuss its validity, strong points, limitations, etc. Your reader will want to know what is at the heart of your thoughts. To analyze, one has to work with a keen mind, knowing precisely how to break things down and where to break them open. After scrutinizing the data, you can interpret. You interpret data by discussing what its appearance means or implies.

Consequently, when you can analyze and interpret you can formulate ideas. Ideas are more fool-proof than notions and opinions. They provide stronger intellectual stimulation and command more respect. Holding these distinctions in mind should arouse your ambition to reach a level of dealing with ideas.

WHAT IS A GOOD WAY TO STRENGTHEN THE CLARITY OF YOUR WRITING?

One way to enforce clarity in your writing is to think,

write and re-write as if you are preparing your manuscript to be translated by another person into a foreign language.

Whenever you can, always if possible, allow your writing to rest for a space of time: hours, days or weeks. When you go back to it, you can read it with a fresh impression. You will have a clearer sense of whether you have been totally successful.

Good knowledge of the subject matter, a thorough examination of it, and clear focus on the issue at hand will help you to write with a style in which your words are discriminating, your phrases crisp and your sentence structure clear.

WHAT IS FLUENCY?

By fluency is meant a freedom and flow of expression in which one demonstrates or exercises mental agility in being able to reveal his or her thoughts or feelings. Producing the good essay is a matter of achieving fluency in the expression of your thought.

HOW CAN YOU ACHIEVE FLUENCY?

Start by being in touch with yourself. Read the good writers you like most. Let these writers stimulate your spirit so that you can better perceive and release the creative rhythm or life-flow best suited to yourself and your particular subject.

Remember that your sense of rhythm, or flow of life, is an important part of your identity. Cultivate it. Don't stifle it if you wish to build a good writing style. Writing is the release of your thought energy. You must activate that energy, and you must control its flow.

Fluent communication is the good ordering of thought and energy. Being in touch with yourself and your subject are your best assets for becoming fluent.

WHAT ARE THE REQUIREMENTS FOR EFFECTIVE PERFORMANCE IN WRITING?

Allowing adequate time to reflect on your subject or letting the subject have the opportunity to become a part of you before you attempt to produce the final product, will eliminate many fundamental difficulties of unity, clarity, order and coherence in your product. Unity, clarity, order and coherence are essential to good writing of any type.

Living with your subject through reflection and note-taking, in addition to reading about it, should provide enough stimulation and creativity within you that you will always be conscious of your engagement in a living process.

WHAT ARE THE BEST WAYS FOR GETTING STARTED ON A WRITING PROJECT?

Getting started can be a big problem at times. When there is this difficulty, you should work by brainstorming. That is, write down all your responses to your subject. Examine what you have put on paper and divide it into categories. Eliminate points not pertinent to your task. After every brainstorming session, you will probably discover that you have more to write about than you thought. You will also find as you examine what you have put on paper that your essay is beginning to organize itself. In addition, you will be made aware of possible weaknesses and strengths.

When you have thought enough about your subject, you can begin to introduce it to your reader. Before introducing the subject in writing to your reader, you should write it out for yourself. This means that rewriting is essential to sharpening your writing skills.

When you finish drafting the body of your paper, you may realize that the introduction and body do not exactly fit. In developing the body you might have struck upon a new and pertinent idea which goes beyond the range of your introduction. In such instances adjustments must be made.

HOW CAN YOU BEST JUDGE YOUR READINESS TO BEGIN A WRITING PROJECT?

An introduction presents your conclusion about a particular subject. If you have reached the point at which you are prepared to present a formulated idea or conclusion, then you must also be prepared to defend that idea or conclusion. If you cannot offer a substantial defense, you are probably not ready to begin. If you have run out of time, you must make the presentation as best as you can.

WHAT IS NOTETAKING, AND WHAT ARE ITS BENEFITS?

Some essay tasks require a great deal of notetaking. This is especially true of essays to be based on materials outside your own consciousness such as research papers. Notetaking is a form of brainstorming, except that you are simply storming someone else's brain as well as your own. Thus, you want to make notes of what they said, how they said it, and where they said it. This is important for giving proper credit to someone else's thoughts, and it is important for helping you to establish, stimulate, and be clear about your own line of thinking.

WHAT IS AN OUTLINE, AND WHAT ARE ITS BENEFITS?

To achieve effective organization and development, your essay should be outlined in your head or on paper. The outline will serve as a roadmap, indicating the route you plan to take and the stops to be made in order to reach your point of destination.

WHAT IS AN INTRODUCTION, AND WHY DO YOU NEED ONE?

When you do not provide an introduction stating the concern or theme of your essay and its scope, you may very well not end up with an essay but a loose association of details. If you establish, clearly and strongly, a conceptual framework for your presentation from the outset, you will find it easier to organize and bring out the points of relation among the ideas or elements you need to discuss. Also, it cannot be overstated that the more familiar you are with the subject matter and its relationship to the writing task at hand, the greater will be your confidence in writing about that material. Your fluency with language should also be greater because you can set forth your thoughts with greater ease, and, therefore, a smoother rhythm. Uncertainty with your material will cause trepidation, which can certainly affect your style.

Since what you present to your reader is what you have already thought out or investigated, your introduction to your subject should include at least one sentence which specifically states your conclusion, major speculations, or point of view. This sentence will be your thesis statement. This statement will set the focus of your presentation. It should also raise your own sense of awareness and commitment to your subject.

WHAT ARE THE BENEFITS OF A GOOD INTRODUCTION?

Inherent to the good introduction is also a clear sense of organization, as well as a clear sense of the range of the essay.

Good organization of the parts is essential. The form certainly can affect the content. Just as a horse has to be bridled to be controlled, so must you control your mental energy as you attempt to manifest it in ideas. It is one thing to feel the potency of your mind, but it is quite another to accept the challenge to convert that potency into the sheer strength of communicable thought. If others are to understand what you feel and think and how you feel and think, then you must organize and master, as much as you can, what it is you wish to communicate.

WHAT IS RE-WRITING?

Re-writing is no more than re-engagement with the scrutinized original product. If you have not scrutinized the original product, there is no need to try to re-write it. When we scrutinize, the problems can become concrete and specific. The reluctance to re-write is a primary handicap to effective writing. Organized and responsible reading, good notetaking, judicious initial interpretation, and considerable reflection upon the subject will eliminate much of the reluctance often encountered at the re-writing stage.

HOW CAN YOU SURMOUNT SPECIFIC PROBLEMS LIKE WRITER'S – BLOCK?

There will be times when you will seem to be speeding ahead, but there will also be encounters with roadblocks. Nearly all roadblocks can be gotten around by asking two questions. The first is: Why am I at this point? When you have determined the nature of the roadblock and accepted the fact of its existence, then you can proceed to the second basic question: How do I get around the roadblock?

At least part of the answer to the second question should

be contained in what you have considered to be the nature of the roadblock itself. To scrutinize your work means you have to scrutinize yourself. Have you thought enough about your subject? Have you read enough? Have you included too much information? Have you arranged the material in its most effective order for this particular writing project? Are you presenting the information clearly? Are the points you are making about the information clear? Are you making all the necessary points about the information?

WHAT ABOUT THE TIME IT TAKES TO WRITE?

You probably will not be able to produce an entire essay in one sitting, but you may produce some great parts of it. Time yourself not so much by minutes but by spaces of time required to draft different sections of your essay. Once you get to the final draft you may very well be able to produce it in one sitting.

WHAT IS THE BEST PROCEDURE TO USE WHEN YOU ARE SHORT OF TIME?

We often use our lack of time as the excuse for the poor quality of our written work. However, it is precisely when we lack what we might consider adequate time that we should be sure that we employ the recommended techniques; for this is the moment of the greatest risks. When time is short, you want to be able to gain the maximal amount of effectiveness from the minimal amount of time you do have.

III

ESSENTIAL TERMINOLOGY AND ELEMENTS IN ESSAY WRITING

WHAT IS DICTION?

Diction relates to word choice. Be selective and discriminating with words. For example, do not use the word *hate* if the quality you really mean is *resentment*.

WHAT IS SYNTAX?

Syntax relates to the arrangement of words in the sentence.

WHAT IS PUNCTUATION?

A *Punctuation mark* generally signifies stops, pauses, stresses and pitches needed to convey and clarify meanings and to separate thoughts.

WHAT IS GRAMMAR?

Grammar refers to all the elements of language (nouns,

verbs, prepositions, conjunctions, adjectives, adverbs, pronouns, and articles, all generally referred to as the eight parts of speech) and how these elements function in relation to each other in a sentence to communicate thought.

WHAT IS A SENTENCE?

A *sentence* is a thought stated by declaration, interrogation, command, or exclamation.

WHAT IS A PARAGRAPH?

A *paragraph* is a cluster of sentences forming a unit which develops a certain aspect of a thought.

WHAT IS AN ESSAY?

By definition, the essay as a form of writing is an attempt to express, generally in prose, one's thoughts upon a particular subject. An essay is a cluster of paragraphs which fulfills, by discussion or elaboration, the development of a thought.

Our word *essay* was first introduced as a literary label by the French writer Michel de Montaigne who published some of his prose reflections under the title *Essais* in 1580.

Essays can be characterized as employing four general modes of discourse or orientation. These modes are the narrative, descriptive, expository, and argumentative. (See pages 26-29 for examples of these modes). These modes may be used separately or in combination depending on the particular inclination and needs of the writer and the requirements of his or her subject.

WHAT ARE THE BROADEST CATEGORIES OF ESSAYS?

The two broadest categories of essays are the informal or personal essay and the formal. The informal or personal essay tends to be less objective. The formal essayist in our times feels more obliged to lay out his reasoning to his audience; that is, to give evidence and consider opinions other than his or her own.

The more formal essay is generally prefered or simply expected in the academic setting unless otherwise requested. This is not an arbitrary decision made by the professor as such, but is more a matter related to the development of one's intellectual faculties toward sound thinking. The sound thinker should want to see the degree to which his or her opinions are valid and the extent to which those opinions are worthy of being retained. This can only be achieved when opinions are scrutinized, and the writers involvement in the process of scrutinization leads to comparing his or her opinions to the opinions of other people.

WHAT ARE THE BASIC MODES OR FORMS OF DISCOURSE IN WHICH ESSAYS ARE WRITTEN?

The four basic *modes of discourse* or forms of communication are *narrative, descriptive, expository* and *argumentative.*

Narration sets forth a sequence of events.

Examples: **On the 28th of October, Kutuzov took his army across to the left bank of the Danube, and then for the first time halted, leaving the Danube between his army and the greater part of the enemy's forces.**

Leo Tolstoy, *War and Peace,*
Modern Library Editions.

Conrad's life now underwent a conspicuous change. In place of his lonely existence under the tutelage of his grief-stricken, dying father, he attended school and experienced the daily companionship of children his own age.

—Bernard C. Myer, Joseph Conrad, Princeton University Press, 1967.

Description depicts or designates the quality of things and actions.

Examples: There is a fascinating girl working behind the counter of this bookstore. She is not at all pretty, her body and arms are thin and overlong, but there is something secret about her face.

—James Alan McPherson, "Just Enough for the City," Elbow Room, Fawcett Books, 1975.

But Webster is not satisfied to rehearse these stock themes; he also feels a responsibility to dispose of certain "idle prejudices" against railroads. Some he dismisses quickly. In one sentence he brushes aside the charge that the new companies are undemocratic, monopolistic, closed corporations.

—Leo Marx, The Machine In the Garden, Oxford University Press, 1969.

Exposition explains. It makes plain the nature, form or function of something—a concept, idea, thing, etc.

Examples: We are slowly becoming aware of what is happening to our environment. More and more individuals and groups speak out against the destruction of the natural world. But as yet we do not see that this destruction has an imperative logic behind it.

—Charles Reich, *The Greening of America,* Bantam, 1971.

The proof is ample, that Beethoven was already fully convinced of the entire innocence of both Prince Kinsky and Prince Lobkowitz of all desire to escape any really just demands upon them. . .

—Elliot Forbes, *Thayer's Life of Beethoven,* Princeton University Press, 1970.

Mother goddesses are earthy goddesses, fertile like the soil. They bring forth new life and nurture it. It was this life-creating power of woman, an elemental force, that filled man with admiration. And this is exactly where problems arise.

—Karen Horney, *Feminine Psychology,* Norton Library 1967.

Argumentation defends or counters an assertion. You have to be so alert in laying out an argument that you may need to use narration, description and exposition to argue your point.

An argumentative essay does not simply involve giving your point of view. It involves explaining and defending your point of view rigorously and vigorously. You not only have to know what you are thinking, but you have to anticipate what your probable opponent is thinking as well. The best argument covers its own territory and keeps an eye on the opposing territory too. Often through ingenuity, you may even be able to convert your opponents ammunition for your own use. (For an example, see Appendix A.)

HOW CAN ONE SEE THESE FOUR MODES AT WORK?

An example of an argumentative essay by American statesman Frederick Douglass, along with an excerpt from the letter that provoked it, is printed in Appendix A in its entirety. It is an excellent example of *argumentation,* demonstrating how Douglass uses *narration, description* and *exposition* all so well to make and defend his point. It would be beneficial if you would read and study this fine piece of writing several times. Examine its various sections to understand more of how Douglass is able to write with such clarity, precision, logic, persuasiveness and confidence.

WHAT ARE THE BENEFITS OF THE COMPARISON-CONTRAST TECHNIQUES WHEN WORKING WITH THE FOUR MODES OF DISCOURSE?

The comparison and contrast technique can be of valuable service when working in either of the four modes of discourse. You may use the comparison and contrast technique implicitly or explicitly to sharpen yours and your reader's insight into the subject considered.

An essay which has as its focus a comparison or contrast treatment should not begin by dealing with one aspect of the comparison or contrast independently of the other aspects. The beginning of the essay should be a comprehensive introductory remark which reveals what you have discovered about your subjects as they stand in relation to each other. This type of opening is vital to the reader's understanding of the nature, scope, focus and direction of your essay. It will attract the reader's attention and help to form his criteria for judging your presentation. When the elements to be compared and contrasted have been adequately introduced, you may give them individual attention. However, you must never forget that to compare and to contrast imply addressing the relationships which exist among elements, whether the relationships point to similarities or differences. Consequently, no element in the discussion should be left standing on its own. You must show how it is similar or dissimilar to other elements of your discussion.

IV

PUNCTUATION AND OTHER
BASIC RULES OF
MECHANICS

WHAT ARE RULES AND EXAMPLES FOR PUNCTUATING
WITH THE COMMA, SEMI-COLON, AND COLON?

THE COMMA—
The *comma* (,) is especially used to mark off interruptive or parenthetical clauses, independent clauses joined
by coordinating conjunctions, clauses standing in opposition,
introductory clauses, adjectives in succession, words, phrases
and sometimes clauses in a series, clauses standing in negation
and non-restrictive modifiers.

Comma: (marks off items in a series)
Strokes or injuries to the left temporal or parietal
lobes of the neocortex often impair the ability to
read, write, speak and perform mathematical
operations. —Howard Rheingold and
Howard Levine, *Talking Tech,*
Wm. Morrow and Co., 1982.

Comma: (marks off the independent clause joined

by the coordinating conjunction *but*)

Not only do our history courses terminate with the year they are taught, but the same situation exists in the study of government and economics, psychology and biology.

—Ossip Flechtheim, *The Futurist,* 1968

Comma: (marks off interruptive or parenthetical clauses)

And now, with something of the terror of the destructive child, he saw himself on the point of inheriting his own destruction.

—D. H. Lawrence, *Women in Love,* Viking Portable Library, 1947

Comma: (marks off independent clauses joined by the coordinating conjunction *or*)

By good fortune she had a veil on her bonnet, or she could hardly have gone along the streets without being stopped.

—Charles Dickens, *A Tale of Two Cities,* Oxford University Press, 1949

Comma: (marks off clauses standing in opposition, i.e. clauses of explanation or specificity)

It was one of the nights in the rainy season in March, the four and twentieth year of my first setting foot in this island of solitariness.

—Daniel Defoe, *Robinson Crusoe,* New American Library, 1961

Three dispositions lead to hell: vanity, avarice and vengeance.

Choose one of the following: the house, boat, or car.

HAT ARE OTHER BASIC RULES OF MECHANICS?

Use *hash (/)* marks to separate two or more lines of etry when written out of their verse form. For example:

> Attend my lays, ye ever honored Nine, / Assist my labors and my strains refine; / In smoothest numbers pour the notes along /
> —Phillis Wheatley, "A Hymn to the Morning," *The Poems of Phillis Wheatley*, University of North Carolina Press, 1966

Enclose titles of poems, essays, short stories, songs, d articles in quotation marks.

Underline book titles, titles of magazines, newspapers, urnals, and epic poems.

Comma: (marks off introductory clauses and adjectives in succession)
Looked at in that way, only **three points** represented real, practical steps toward a new corrections system rather than a tardy effort **to reach a bare minimum standard of decency in the treatment of human beings temporarily confined.**
> —Tom Wicker, *A Time to Die,* Quadrangle, The New York Times Book Co., 1975

Firmly and unhesitatingly he bore witness that the sum spent a month before could not have been less than three thousand, that all the peasants about here would testify that they had heard the sum of three thousand mentioned by Dmitri Fyordorovitch himself.
> —Fyodor Dostoevsky, *The Brothers Karamazov,* Vintage Books, 1955

Comma: (marks off a dependent clause serving as modifier)
Somebody had him by the collar with one hand, slapping him around with the other.
> —Ernest Gaines, *Of Love and Dust,* W. W. Norton, 1967

Comma: (marks off the clause standing in negation)
It is implied in the very nature of the institution, the aim of which is to make the economic and sexual union of man and woman serve the interest of society, not assure their personal happiness.
> —Simone de Beauvoir, *The Second Sex,* Vintage, 1974

Comma: (marks off the non-restrictive modifier, a modifier which adds to the meaning of a noun or verb without attempting to limit that noun or verb)

The world has been instructed by its kings, who have so magnetized the eyes of nations.

—Ralph Waldo Emerson,
"Self-Reliance," *Selections
From Ralph Waldo Emerson,*
Houghton Mifflin, 1957

Comma: (marks off the independent clause joined by the coordinating conjunction *and*)

All the rest is a lie, and my midwife's resolve to oppose the lie arises through anger and love.

—Cecil Williams, *I'm Alive!,*
Harper and Row, 1980

THE SEMICOLON—

The *semicolon (;)* is used to separate clauses joined by conjunctive adverbs (however, moreover, nevertheless, consequently, etc.); to clarify sections which contain smaller units in which several commas have already been used; and to indicate equanimity between independent clauses in a sentence not joined by a conjunction.

Oedipus did not remember the thongs that bound his feet; nevertheless the marks they left testified to that doom toward which his feet were leading him.

—James Baldwin, "Many
Thousands Gone," *Notes of a
Native Son,* Beacon Press,
1955

34

Half the contents of the newspaper d⟨
tics, in one way or another; entries
catalog run to seven pages; every c⟨
world has a political system; and poli
ments, presumably, have existed s
government began.

—Gregory Cowa
Elisabeth McPh⟨
English Rhetori⟨
2nd ed., Rando⟨

For herself, she lingered in the sour
room long after the fire had gone ou⟨
danger of her feeling cold; she was ir

—Henry James,
of a Lady, New
Library, 1963

THE COLON—

The *colon (:)* is a mark indicating that su
information—generally of explanation, specifi⟨
struction—will follow.

But one must ask: What is this self
self? Radical Existentialism answers
of itself.

—Paul Tillich,
To Be, Yale Ur
1962

He was quite calm: his heart beat e
of a man resolved upon a dangerou
undertaking.

—Alexander Pu
The Queen of
Penguin Book⟨

35

V
DOCUMENTATION OF SOURCES:
REFERENCE CITATIONS
(Footnotes, Endnotes, and Bibliographies)

The *reference citation* is used by the writer to inform the reader of the particular source from which the writer's information and thoughts are being drawn.

In its most basic sense, the reference citation indicates the place to which the reader may look to find the origin of the writer's information, the stimulus for the writer's thinking and discussion, or to find a more detailed discussion of the issues presented. In its most complete and appreciable form, the reference citation specifically informs the reader of the name of the author of the book or article from which the writer's thoughts and information are being drawn; it gives the title, place of publication, date of publication (including year, month, and day in the case of articles), the page number(s), and the volume number if there is more than one volume.

Not only printed materials but also speeches, lectures, radio and television broadcasts, private discussions, or interviews, etc. can be used as reference materials. Yet, these sources, too, need to be given specific documentation, indicating to the reader the author, title, place, and date of the occurrence of this particular type of source or reference.

Your reference citation is important to the reader not simply as a validation of your thoughts but because the thoughts you present about a subject or issue may not be wholly your own. While every thought does not have to have another thinker as its source, when you use any type of information which is not common knowledge (historical, sociological, psychological, philosophical, scientific, etc. to which you were not privy as a participant or observer or of which you are not the originator), then it is important for you to provide a reference.

The reference helps to give credibility to your information and thoughts; it helps to strengthen and encourage belief in your arguments. In addition, the reference citation is very important because it allows the interested reader to check to see whether you are doing justice to the material which you are using or interpreting. Moreover, the use of the reference citation is the expected, professional way of giving credit to the authors whose materials have helped you to accomplish your goal of organizing and presenting your discussion.

To give credit to those authors and works which have been of assistance to you is not only an academic matter. In academic institutions and professional life, this is an ethical matter, a question of right and wrong, of intellectual honesty and theft. If you draw upon the ideas of others without giving credit, then you will be judged as dishonest. If you use the exact words of someone else without giving credit by placing those words within quotation marks, you will be judged as dishonest.

This type of dishonesty is called *plagiarism*. Plagiarism is an infraction or violation which should not be taken lightly. The penalties for acts of plagiarism can indeed be costly. Individual institutions usually set their own penalties for plagiarism. Some institutions authorize the professor to fail the student on the particular assignment which shows evidence of plagiarism; some authorize the professor to fail the student for the entire course; yet there have been times when schools have also dismissed students from their programs for acts of plagiarism.

Professional and public careers have been damaged and ruined as a result of acts of plagiarism. Professors have resigned from the most distinguished universities, and noted authors have been sued for plagiarism. Therefore, it is important, *for your own safety,* to make formal acknowledgement of your sources.

STYLES OF DOCUMENTATION

There are several standard styles of documentation which are adequate for most purposes. Some authors, journals, professors, and disciplines prefer one style over the other, however. Two of the standard styles used in the United States are the Modern Language Association (MLA) style and the Chicago style. Thus, if you would look in the front of any major scholarly journal (which always requires documentation in its articles), you will find a prescribed style requested by the journal for the articles which are submitted to its editors. For example, inside the front cover of the journal CULTURAL CRITIQUE, you will find the statement: "Contributors should submit two copies of manuscript conforming to THE CHICAGO MANUAL OF STYLE (13th Ed.; ch. 17)...."

Most of the information found in composition texts or manuals concerning the writing of research and term papers, theses, and dissertations is drawn from the MLA or Chicago manuals of style. When writing a documented presentation, you should be consistent and use only one mode of documentation.

TYPES OF CITATIONS

A. *The footnote:* this was among the oldest and most popularly used forms of citation until the 1960s. This form of citation was called a "footnote" because it appeared at the bottom of the page. This form was so pervasive that the word "footnote" has virtually become a synonym or generic word for reference citation itself.

B. *The in-text, internal or parenthetical note:* this is a very succinct citation which appears within the discussion itself, immediately following the material which requires the reference.

C. *The endnote:* this style of citation is very much like the footnote in its form but is placed at the end of the chapter in assembly with other citations for that chapter, or may be placed in a section for "chapter endnotes" at the back of a book-length study.

D. *The bibliography:* the word "bibliography" refers to a compilation of the basic texts (including books, articles, lectures, interviews, etc.) which the writer used or drew upon in developing the presentation. A standard bibliography entry gives the reader everything found in the general footnote entry except that the page numbers from *non-periodical* texts are left off. A more recent form of the bibliographic compilation which now has great currency is labeled "Works Cited" or "Selected Bibliography." Professors will inform you when they have particular preferences for the form of the bibliography.

For further reference, three excellent, readily available manuals which you may use to learn virtually all the details of documentation beyond the information and examples given in this book are:

Gibaldi, Joseph and Walter S. Achtert. MLA HANDBOOK FOR WRITERS OF RESEARCH PAPERS. 3rd. ed. New York: The Modern Language Association of America, 1988.

- - - - - - - - - - - - . THE MLA STYLE MANUAL. New York: The Modern Language Association of America, 1985.

Lester, James D. WRITING RESEARCH PAPERS: A COMPLETE GUIDE. 4th ed. Glenview: Scott, Foresman and Company, 1984.

Other specialized style manuals for various disciplines include the following:

American Chemical Society. HANDBOOK FOR AUTHORS OF PAPERS IN AMERICAN CHEMICAL SOCIETY PUBLICATIONS. Washington: American Chemical Society, 1978.

American Institute of Physics. Publications Board. STYLE MANUAL FOR GUIDANCE IN THE PREPARATION OF PAPERS. 3rd ed. New York: American Institute of Physics, 1978.

American Mathematical Society. A MANUAL FOR AUTHORS OF MATHEMATICAL PAPERS. 8th. ed. Providence: American Mathematical Society, 1984.

American Psychological Association. PUBLICATION MAN-
UAL OF THE AMERICAN PSYCHOLOGICAL
ASSOCIATION. 3rd ed. Washington: American Psycho-
logical Association, 1983.

Council of Biology Editors. Style Manual Committee. CBE
STYLE MANUAL: A GUIDE FOR AUTHORS, EDI-
TORS, AND PUBLISHERS IN THE BIOLOGICAL
SCIENCES. 5th ed. Bethesda: Council of Biology Edi-
tors, 1983.

(Note: You may consult your Reference Librarian for similar
style manuals pertaining to other disciplines, or see John Bruce
Howell, STYLE MANUALS OF THE ENGLISH-SPEAKING
WORLD (Phoenix: Oryx, 1983).

POINTS TO CONSIDER WHEN PREPARING THE CITATIONAL AND BIBLIOGRAPHIC ENTRIES

Certain particulars should always be considered when
preparing an entry. Details of the bibliographic entries should
be arranged in your entry with respect to the following order:
(1)   The name of the author of the information.
(2)   The title of the particular article, speech, etc. if the text
        is part of a larger anthology, magazine, etc.
(3)   The title of the volume in which the particular text is
        found.
(4)   The name of the translator if one is involved.
(5)   The name of the editor if your text is part of an
        anthology.
(6)   The edition of the work if there has been more than one.
(7)   The number of the volume if the work used is part of a
        series of volumes such as journals, encyclopedias, or

other multi-volume works.

(8)   The name of the series if there is such.

(9)   The place of publication, name of publisher, and date of publication.

(10)   The page numbers of the particular pages from which information has been drawn.

(11)   Additional information such as original publication date of a reprinted work and your personal comments about the work, if important.

SAMPLES

Following are two examples of textual and bibliographic documentation. The first is done in accordance with the intext-author-date system, and the second is done in accordance with the endnote system. For the easiest comparative purposes of seeing the difference between the two systems, I will use one sample text for illustration. The rules are drawn from THE CHICAGO MANUAL OF STYLE and THE MLA STYLE MANUAL cited above. These two systems are among the most preferred by scholarly editors and publishers. Both the University of Chicago Press and the Modern Language Association strongly encourage the use of the intext-author-date system. The MLA prefers the intext-author-date system exclusively for its publications.

The basic form of the *intext-author-date* system consists of two essential parts. The first is placed in parenthesis immediately following the referenced information and is composed of the last name(s) of the author(s), the year of publication, the volume (when applicable), and the page number, respectively. For example, then, an intext-author-date reference to this book would be (Peters 1990, 54). Such a citation is a code which the reader can use to find the complete information about the work, listed in the "Bibliography" or "Works Cited" section at the end of the presentation, which composes the second part of this system. This compilation of references should be listed alphabetically by the last name of the authors. Study the following example.

THE BACKGROUND OF THE RAP MUSIC POETRY OF THE 1980s

The rap music poetry of the 1980s has a deeply rooted tradition in Afro-American culture. Rapping is a cherished Afro-American verbal ritual which is used especially to demonstrate one's oral linguistic proficiency. The rap is generally very spectacular, dramatic, and highly stylized. Its function is to impress while conveying information (Smitherman 1973, 262). A very important antecedent of rap music poetry is the Afro-American jive tradition which was cultivated to a high level of maturity in the 1940s, during the childhood years of the parents of many of the rap music artists. In fact, an entire book was written on the language of jive during that period (Dundes, 1973, 206). The characteristics which Arna Bontemps and Langston Hughes find in jive language show an obvious kinship to features of rap music poetry. Bontemps and Hughes find in jive language great flexibility and an infinite capacity for phrasing that expresses "rare harmonic beauty and rhythmical force" (Bontemps and Hughes, 1958, 479). For them jive language is constantly increased with descriptive phrasing which is both "narrative and explanatory in content," and it is marked by "experimentation in rhymes"

(Bontemps and Hughes, 480).

The general rap tradition has several well-known characteristics. There is often a great deal of exaggeration or hyperbole which may be coupled with a great deal of braggadocio or boasting. There is often a great deal of mimicry. Proverbial statements may be used throughout the speaker's talk in order to give himself an air of sagacity and dominance. The strategy of punning is frequently employed. There is a preponderance of creative image-making. Moreover, the power of the rap is grounded in regenerative expression in which the familiar and even the trivial is given new metaphorical strength (Smitherman 1977, 94-100).

Rap music poetry of the 1980s is often characterized by a rapid meter with weighty, staccato-paced lines, measured rhythmic beats, terse cadences, and is replete with terminal rhyme and emphatic caesurae. 1980s rap music poetry is also marked by rhythmic force and verbal virtuosity. Thus, according to David Sargent, it most often "consists of a steady stream of rhymed couplets, meant to suggest the illusion of on-the-spot improvisation even though they are more carefully planned in advance" (Sargent 1981, 91). Rap music poetry of the 1980s is described by Steven Dougherty as "raw street poetry" set "to a booming beat" (Dougherty 1986, 58). Nancy Griffin depicts rap as "music with a simple, funky beat and chanted lyrics that tell stories often about romantic prowess" (Griffin 1983, 162). Rap music poetry "uses rhythmic chanting over repetitive, minimalist backing tracks . . . , " says Peg Tyre writing in NEW YORK magazine (Tyre 1968, 14). Rap music poetry may also employ other standard Afro-American elements such as the refrain and the call-response techniques. In the tradition of earlier forms of rapping, the overall tone and style of 1980s rap music poetry reflects a sense of "assertiveness, display, pride, status and competition," argue the music critics of TIME magazine (TIME, 21 March 1983, 72).

WORKS CITED

Bontemps, Arna and Hughes, Langston. THE BOOK OF NEGRO FOLK-LORE. New York: Dodd, Mead and Company, 1958.

Burley, Dan. "The Technique of Jive." MOTHER WIT FROM THE LAUGHING BARREL. Ed. Alan Dundes. Englewood Cliffs: Prentice-Hall, Inc., 1973.

"Chilling Out On Rap Flash." TIME 21 March 1983: 72.

Dougherty, Steven. "L. L. Cool J Raps to the Beat of His Box, While His LP Does Better Than Dow Jones Stocks." PEOPLE WEEKLY MAGAZINE 21 April 1986: 58.

Griffin, Nancy. "Rap Zaps America." LIFE January 1983: 162.

Sargent, David. "The Real Roots of Mainstream Pop? 'Rap''s Rhythms." VOGUE September 1981: 91.

Smitherman, Geneva. "The Power of the Rap: The Black Idiom and the New Black Poetry." TWENTIETH CENTURY LITERATURE 19 (1973): 262.

- - - - - - - - - - . TALKIN AND TESTIFYIN. Boston: Houghton Mifflin Co., 1977.

Tyre, Peg. "Rap Stars." NEW YORK 11 August 1986: 14.

The basic form of the *endnote* specifies the name of the author, place of publication, publisher, year of publication, page number(s), and other relevant details as itemized in the enumerated stipulations above. A superscript (raised arabic number) is the code which is placed immediately following the reference information to signal to the reader where in the endnotes to find the relevant citation.

When making repeated references to pages of a text, or when the author of the text has been made clear for the reader, it is recommended that you give only one endnote citation coded by superscript. Thereafter, give the page numbers to that text within your discussion in parenthesis (e.g. 17-19) immediately following the reference information. Thus, the first endnote for the repeated reference may read:

1. Unless otherwise stated, the poetry of Gwendolyn Brooks is quoted from SELECTED POEMS (New York: Harper and Row, 1963; and that of Gary Soto from THE ELEMENTS OF SAN JOAQUIN (Pittsburgh: The University of Pittsburgh Press, 1977).

In addition, you may include in the endnote, following the basic citation information, any significant comment about the relative value of the material being used. Study the changes made below to the essay example on rap music.

THE BACKGROUND OF THE RAP MUSIC POETRY OF THE 1980s

The rap music poetry of the 1980s has a deeply rooted tradition in Afro-American culture. Rapping is a cherished Afro-American verbal ritual which is used especially to demonstrate one's oral linguistic proficiency. The rap is generally very spectacular, dramatic, and highly stylized. Its function is to impress while conveying information.[1] A very important antecedent of rap music poetry is the Afro-American jive tradition which was cultivated to a high level of maturity in the 1940s, during the childhood years of the parents of many of the rap music artists. In fact, an entire book was written on the language of jive during that period.[2] The characteristics which Arna Bontemps and Langston Hughes find in jive language show an obvious kinship to features of rap music poetry. Bontemps and Hughes find in jive language great flexibility and an infinite capacity for phrasing that expresses "rare harmonic beauty and rhythmical force."[3] Jive language is constantly increased with descriptive phrasing which is both "narrative and explanatory in content," and it is marked by "experimentation in rhymes."[4]

The general rap tradition has several well-known characteristics. There is often a great deal of exaggeration or hyperbole which may be coupled with a great deal of braggadocio or boasting. There is often a great deal of mimicry. Proverbial statements may be used throughout the speaker's talk in order to give himself an air of sagacity and dominance. The strategy of punning is frequently employed. There is a preponderance of creative image-making. Moreover, the power of the rap is grounded in regenerative expression in which the familiar and even the trivial is given new metaphorical strength.[5]

Rap music poetry of the 1980s is often characterized by a rapid meter with weighty, staccato-paced lines, measured rhythmic beats, terse cadences, and is replete with terminal rhyme and emphatic caesurae. 1980s rap music poetry is also marked by rhythmic force and verbal virtuosity. Thus, according to David Sargent, it most often "consists of a steady stream of rhymed couplets, meant to suggest the illusion of on-the-spot improvisation even though they are more carefully planned in advance."[6] Rap music poetry of the 1980s is described by Steven Dougherty as "raw street poetry" set "to a booming beat."[7] Nancy Griffin depicts rap as "music with a simple, funky beat and chanted lyrics that tell stories, often about romantic prowess."[8] Rap music poetry "uses rhythmic chanting over repetitive, minimalist backing tracks . . . ," says Peg Tyre writing in NEW YORK magazine.[9] Rap music poetry may also employ other standard Afro-American elements such as the refrain and the call-response techniques. In the tradition of earlier forms of rapping, the overall tone and style of 1980s rap poetry reflects a sense of "assertiveness, display, pride, status and competition," argue the music critics of TIME magazine.[10]

ENDNOTES

1. Geneva Smitherman, "The Power of the Rap," TWENTIETH CENTURY LITERATURE 19 (1973): 262.

2. Dan Burley, "The Technique of Jive," MOTHER WIT FROM THE LAUGHING BARREL, ed. Alan Dundes (Englewood Cliffs: Prentice-Hall, 1973) 206.

3. Arna Bontemps and Langston Hughes, THE BOOK OF NEGRO FOLKLORE (New York: Dodd, Mead and Co., 1958) 479.

4. Ibid., 480.

5. Geneva Smitherman, TALKIN AND TESTIFYIN (Boston: Houghton Mifflin Co., 1977) 94-100. This is perhaps the best and most comprehensive study of Afro-American language styles ever published.

6. David Sargent,"The Real Roots of Mainstream Pop? 'Rap''s Rhythms," VOGUE September 1981: 91.

7. Steven Dougherty, "L. L. Cool J Raps to the Beat of His Box, While His LP Does Better Than Dow Jones Stocks," PEOPLE WEEKLY MAGAZINE 21 June 1986: 58.

8. Nancy Griffin, "Rap Zaps America," LIFE January 1983: 162.

9. Peg Tyre, "Rap Stars," NEW YORK 11 August 1986: 14.

10. "Chilling Out On Rap Flash," TIME 21 March 1983: 72.

WORKS CITED

Bontemps, Arna and Hughes, Langston. THE BOOK OF NEGRO FOLKLORE. New York: Dodd, Mead and Company, 1958.

Burley, Dan. "The Technique of Jive." MOTHER WIT FROM THE LAUGHING BARREL. Ed. Alan Dundes. Englewood Cliffs: Prentice-Hall, Inc., 1973.

"Chilling Out On Rap Flash." TIME 21 March 1983: 72.

Dougherty, Steven. "L. L. Cool J Raps to the Beat of His Box, While His LP Does Better Than Dow Jones Stocks." PEOPLE WEEKLY MAGAZINE 21 April 1986: 58.

Griffin, Nancy. "Rap Zaps America." LIFE January 1983: 162.

Sargent, David. "The Real Roots of Mainstream Pop? 'Rap' 's Rhythms." VOGUE September 1981: 91.

Smitherman, Geneva. "The Power of the Rap: The Black Idiom and the New Black Poetry." TWENTIETH CENTURY LITERAUTRE 19 (1973): 262.

- - - - - - - - - - - . TALKIN AND TESTIFYIN. Boston: Houghton Mifflin Co., 1977.

Tyre, Peg. "Rap Stars." NEW YORK 11 August 1986: 14.

One other stylistic point to remember is that when you quote a phrase, sentence, or paragraph you should refer to the author of that quotation by name when the name is known. Your reader can be thrown off cue and can lose the logic of your thought progression if you quote anonymously.

The documentation process always involves giving attention to details. It is best therefore that you follow the rules and be patient with yourself as you learn the various documentation systems necessary for carrying out your work.

VI
WRITING THE
BOOK REVIEW ESSAY

WHAT IS A BOOK REVIEW

A book review is a critical summary of a book you have read or have reasonably familiarized yourself with. It is very important to remember that the book review is not the same as the book report. The book review essay is an exercise in critical reading and succinct, discriminating and interpretative or analytic writing. The book review is fundamentally analytical and evaluative; whereas, the book report is mostly summary with less attention given to critical evaluation.

Published reviews are generally written by people with a particular expertise or who have reasonable acquaintance with the area of discipline with which the book is concerned. Yet, as constant readers of books, we are all reviewers, whether we have developed and refined our skills or not. Without doubt we all have some opinions, notions, feelings, or thoughts about every book we handle (novels, telephone books, dictionaries, magazines, etc.), even though we may not have crystallized these thoughts in our minds.

If you are to be a good reviewer, you must function as a competent and reliable guide who helps your audience to decide upon the merit of the book in question. Depending upon the competence with which you write, you may be the sole determinant of whether the audience feels the book warrants its attention.

The competent reviewer is usually well-versed in the background of the subject which is treated in the selected work. However, if you are working in a relatively new or foreign area, you may still write an interesting or provocative review. But in this case you must be sure to approach the subject out of your own innocence. A pretentious handling of the subject matter will lead more to a revelation of your shortcomings as a reviewer than to the merits or short-comings of the book itself.

If you have not been assigned a specific book to review, it will probably serve the best interest of yourself and your essay to select a work to which you are reasonably certain you can give your attention. Your choice may be determined by your familiarity with a certain author, subject, or written form (e.g.: autobiography, biography, fiction, poetry, drama, history, criticism, reference, etc.).

When beginning to write the review, you should be specific in your opening about the subject of the book, its author, and its general classification as a written form. You must remember that your foremost concern is with communicating the book's purpose and in evaluating how well and by what means the purpose was executed. It cannot be over-emphasized that in writing the book review, you must be especially careful not to try to present every detail which is provided in the book. Neither should you attempt to retell the fiction writer's story. A summary of the book is an important element of the essay, but it should not occupy more than one-quarter of the space given to critical interpretation and evaluation. The reviewer's responsibility is to present an informed or, at least, inquisitive perspective on what the author has done. You must summarize, but most of all you must analyze and interpret. From there you can proceed to your own conclusive evaluation.

The reviewer cannot honestly evaluate what he has not read. Thus you cannot make judgements on the whole unless you are reasonably familiar with each part. It is important that you examine preliminaries such as the table of contents and the introduction if you are to become acquainted with the author's intentions and his scope. The nature and complexity of the book itself will usually dictate the amount of attention you as reviewer need to devote to each section.

PROCEDURES AND POINTS TO CONSIDER WHILE UNDERTAKING THE BOOK REVIEW ASSIGNMENT

1. As you read, take notes on all that you think and feel about the information, style or manner of presentation, organization, etc.

2. Think about the book's title and get a sense of the expectations it arouses in you: what does the title suggest the book will be about?

3. Examine the table of contents:
   — Reflect upon each chapter heading.
   — Note the chapters which are especially interesting to you.

4. If this is a book whose general intention appears to be to persuade, explain or disseminate information, be sure to read the preface and the introduction

thoroughly to find the author's specific purpose, or to see if the purpose is clearly stated. This is important because much of your judgement of the book's achievement will be guided by what has been set forth as the author's intent. If the introduction or preface has been written by someone other than the author, what value does this preface or introduction have?

5. If the book is an anthology, does it have a central theme? Is it better in some places than in others? In which and why?

6. Is the treatment of the subject area adequate? Is it better in some places than in others? In which and why.

7. What is the nature of the writing style? Is the language dead or alive or what? Does it vary from chapter to chapter, or from subject to subject?

8. What are the strengths of the book? What specifically is there about the book that holds your attention, or does not hold your attention?

9. How does this work compare with similar texts with which you may be familiar? How does it compare with other works by the same author?

10. If this is a research oriented text, is there adequate documentation in the footnotes and bibliography of the sources of the information from which the author has drawn?

11. If this is a revised edition of the book, how has the book been altered? To what purpose and effect?

12. Would you recommend this book? Under what conditions?

13. If you are not very familiar with the nature and form of the book review, please take the time to consult almost any journal, magazine, or newspaper and read a few.

14. When you begin to write the review, that is, after you have examined the book thoroughly and taken your notes, be sure to give the author, complete title, publisher, publication date, and the book's classification. What we mean by classification is whether the book is fiction, poetry, biography, autobiography, history, reference, criticism or whatever.

15. Remember that the fear of re-writing is a primary handicap to effective writing. Organized and responsible reading, concise notetaking, judicious and accurate interpretation, and considerable reflection upon the materials examined and the conclusions drawn will eliminate much of the fear and, therefore, ineffectiveness.

REFERENCES

Drewry, John E. BOOK REVIEWING. Boston: The Writer, 1945, 1966.

Gard, Wayne. BOOK REVIEWING. New York: Alfred Knopf, 1927.

Jones, Llewellyn. HOW TO CRITICIZE BOOKS. New York: W. W. Norton, 1928.

Mavity, Nancy. THE MODERN NEWSPAPER. New York: Henry Holt and Co., 1930.

Reed, P. E. WRITING JOURNALISTIC FEATURES. New York: McGraw-Hill, Inc., 1931.

Shuman, Edwin. HOW TO JUDGE A BOOK. Boston: Houghton Mifflin, 1910.

VI
CONCLUSION

In conclusion, the good writer is the confident writer. The good writer is confident because s/he has spent time investigating and thinking through his/her subject. The good writer knows that language is his/her birthright, but s/he also knows that s/he must work to open up and refine the channel through which his/her language flows—which is himself or herself.

If you are working with a writing teacher, remember when you are shown errors that it is the teacher's job to assess your level of performance, to sensitize you to your weaknesses and strengths, and to show you what you need to do to become more effective in written communication. The teacher's critical input should stimulate you to take periodic inventory of your skills and your standards.

Periodically, you should take into account where you are, where you have been, and where you need to direct your energies. Criticism can be vital to your growth. Review or think about the weaknesses of previous essays before you start your new ones.

APPENDIX A

FREDERICK DOUGLASS' CORRESPONDENCE WITH H. C. WRIGHT CONCERNING HIS MANUMISSION PAPERS AS AN EXAMPLE OF ARGUMENTATIVE WRITING EMPLOYING OTHER MODES OF DISCOURSE

Pursued by slave-catchers, fugitive bondman Frederick Douglass (1817-1895) had to flee the United States of America where he wanted to remain with his wife and family to continue his work toward the abolition of slavery. In order that he could be free to devote his life to this service, some of Douglass' friends decided to pay Douglass' former master the one-hundred-fifty pounds demanded before he would release Douglass from what he considered his legal claim to Douglass' life.

One friend of Douglass, H. C. Wright, vehemently objected to Douglass' engagement in the transaction. Wright sent his objection to Douglass in England, and in due course Douglass wrote an argumentative reply, which is printed here in full.

Douglass' argumentative letter-essay is a fine example of cogent and fluent thinking and writing. It illustrates the nature, interdependence, and intercooperation between the modes of discourse defined above, as well as the rewards of organized cogent thinking in effective writing.

Because Douglass' argumentative response is written in letter form, it has the quality of the personal, familiar or informal essay. Nevertheless the discussion is carried out with a very high regard for objective reasoning and analysis.

The first two paragraphs function as a general introduction to the concerns of the letter-essay.

H. C. Wright presents the basis of his point of view to Douglass in the following terms*:

As a nation, that confederacy, professing to be based upon the principle, that God made you free, and gave you an inalienable right to liberty, claims a right of property in your body and soul—to turn you into a chattel, a slave, again, at any moment. That claim you denied; the authority and power of the whole nation you spurned and defied, when, by running away, you spurned that miserable wretch, who held you as a slave. It was no longer a contest between you and that praying, psalm-singing slave-breeder, but a struggle between you and 17,000,000 of liberty-loving Republicans. By their laws and constitution, you are not a *freeman*, but a *slave*; you are not a *man*, but a *chattel*. You planted your foot upon their laws and constitution, and asserted your freedom and your manhood. You arraigned your antagonist—the slave-breeding Republic—before the tribunal of mankind, and of God. You have stated your case, and pleaded your cause, as none other could state and plead it. Your position, as the slave of that Republic, as the marketable commodity, the dehumanized, outraged *man* of a powerful nation, whose claim and power over you, you have dared to despise, invests you with influence among all to whom your appeal is made, and gathers around you their deep-felt, absorbing, and efficient sympathy. Your appeal to mankind is not against the grovelling thief, Thomas Auld, but against the more daring, more impudent and potent thief—the Republic of the United States of America. You will lose the advantages of this truly manly, and, to my view, sublime position; you will be shorn of your strength—you will sink in your own estimation, if you accept that detestable certificate of your freedom, that blasphemous forgery, that accursed Bill of Sale of your body and soul; or, even by silence, acknowledge its validity.

---

*The full text of Mr. Wright's letter is available in Carter G. Woodson's *The Mind of the Negro as Reflected In His Letters Written During the Crisis 1800-1860*. Washington, D.C.: The Association For the Study of Negro Life and History Inc, 1926, pp. 448-458.

FREDERICK DOUGLASS' REPLY

22, St. Ann's Square, Manchester, 22d Dec., 1846

Henry C. Wright:

Dear Friend:—Your letter of the 12th December reached me at this place, yesterday. Please accept my heartfelt thanks for it. I am sorry that you deemed it necessary to assure me, that it would be the last letter of advice you would ever write me. It looked as if you were about to cast me off for ever! I do not, however, think you meant to convey any such meaning; and if you did, I am sure you will see cause to change your mind, and to receive me again into the fold of those, whom it should ever be your pleasure to advise and instruct.

The subject of your letter is one of deep importance, and upon which, I have thought and felt much; and, being the party of all others most deeply concerned, it is natural to suppose I have an opinion, and ought to be able to give it on all fitting occasions. I deem this a fitting occasion, and shall act accordingly.

In the *third paragraph* Douglass takes on what he feels is the necessary posture or stance for pursuing his argument. The final sentence of this paragraph is a specific statement of his argumentative position:

You have given me your opinion: I am glad you have done so. You have given it to me direct, in your own emphatic way. You never speak insipidly, smoothly, or mincingly; you have strictly adhered to your custom, in the letter before me. I now take great pleasure in giving you my opinion, as plainly and unreservedly as you have given yours, and I trust with equal good feeling and purity of motive. I take it, that nearly all that can be said against my position is contained in your letter; for if any man in the wide world would be likely to find valid objections to such a transaction as the one under consideration, I regard you as that man. I must, however, tell you, that I have read your letter over, and over again, and have sought in vain to find anything like what I can regard a valid reason *against the purchase of my body, or against my receiving the manumission papers, if they are ever presented to me.*

In the *fourth paragraph* we have the formal initiation of the argument with an indication of Douglass' sense of plan for laying out his argument in stages. We notice that he has a topic sentence followed by some parenthetical information before he proceeds to present his facts.

60

This parenthetical information would not be necessary in a more formal or impersonal essay. But Douglass includes it here because he wants to be careful to preserve a friendship while handling a sensitive subject:

Let me, in the first place, state the facts and circumstances of the transaction which you so strongly condemn. It is your right to do so, and God forbid that I should ever cherish the slightest desire to restrain you in the exercise of that right. I say to you at once, and in all the fulness of sincerity, speak out; speak freely; keep nothing back; let me know your whole mind. 'Hew to the line, though the chips fly in my face.' Tell me, and tell me plainly, when you think I am deviating from the strict line of duty and principle; and when I become unwilling to hear, I shall have attained a character which I now despise, and from which I would hope to be preserved. But to the facts.

Douglass has basically employed the expository mode in his first four paragraphs. In the fifth *paragraph*, he *continues to use the expository mode* to lay out the explanation of his circumstances in direct, concise language, leading us into an understanding of his reasoning about the matter at hand. However, he moves from the use of exposition to the *use of narration* in the second part of the second sentence in this paragraph. Then in the third sentence of the paragraph, he makes *use of the descriptive mode* to present the intentions of his friends engaged in paying the one-hundred-fifty pounds or seven-hundred-fifty dollars to his former master:

I am in England, my family are in the United States. My sphere of usefulness is in the United States; my public and domestic duties are there; and there it seems my duty to go. But I am *legally* the property of Thomas Auld, and if I go the United States, (no matter to what part, for there is no City of Refuge there, no spot sacred to freedom there,) Thomas Auld, *aided by the American Government,* can seize, bind and fetter, and drag me from my family, feed his cruel revenge upon me, and doom me to unending slavery. In view of this simple statement of facts, a few friends, desirous of seeing me released from the terrible liability, and to relieve my wife and children from the painful trepidation, consequent upon the liability, and to place me on an equal footing of safety with all other anti-slavery lecturers in the United States, and to enhance my usefulness by enlarging the field of my labors in the United

States, have nobly and generously paid Hugh Auld, the agent of Thomas Auld, £150—in consideration of which, Hugh Auld (acting as his agent) and the government of the United States agree, that I shall be free from all further liability.

Paragraph six is a transitional paragraph, bringing to conclusion the first segment in Douglass' defense of his position.

Paragraph seven is a further elaboration of Douglass' defense through *exposition,* explaining the motives of his friends.

In *paragraph eight* Douglass shows that he is ready to attack what H. C. Wright proposes as the basic issue—the possible violation by Douglass of moral principles. Douglass *uses exposition* to state his opposing view in precise and clear terms:

These, dear friend, are the facts of the whole transaction. The principle here acted on by my friends, and that upon which I shall act in receiving the manumission papers, I deem quite defensible.

First, *as to those who acted as my friends, and their actions.* The actuating motive was, to secure me from a liability full of horrible forebodings to myself and family. With this object, I will do you the justice to say, I believe you fully unite, although some parts of your letters would seem to justify a different belief.

Then, as to the measure adopted to secure this result. Does it violate a fundamental principle, or does it not? This is the question, and to my mind the only question of importance, involved in the discussion. I believe that, on our part, no just or holy principle has been violated.

In the first three sentences of *paragraph nine,* Douglass uses straightforward expository analysis to undermine H. C. Wright's logic. In the fourth sentence, Douglass *uses the descriptive mode* to implicate H. C. Wright's actions and thereby implicates Wright's moral principles:

Before entering upon the argument in support of this view, I will take the liberty (and I know you will pardon it) to say, I think you should have pointed out some principle violated in the transaction, before you proceeded to exhort me to repentance. You have given me any amount of indignation against 'Auld' and the United States, in all which I cordially unite, and felt refreshed by reading; but it has no bearing whatever upon the conduct of myself, or friends, in the matter under consideration. It does not prove that I have done wrong, nor does it demonstrate what is right, or the proper course to be pursued. Now that the matter has reached its present point, before entering upon the argument, let me say one other word; it is this—I do not think you have acted quite consistently with your character for promptness, in delaying your advice till the transaction was completed. You knew of the movement at its conception, and have known it through its progress, and have never to my knowledge, uttered one syllable against it, in conversation or letter, till now that the deed is done. I regret this, not because I think your earlier advice would have altered the result, but because it would have left me more free than I can now be, since the thing is done. Of course, you will not think hard of my alluding to this circumstance. Now, then, to the main question.

Paragraph ten proceeds mainly by *exposition*. Douglass strengthens the clarity of his expository statement through the use of interrogation, that is, through the raising of a vital question and the answering of the question specifically through itemization. This technique helps him to keep his focus or main line of argument clearly before himself and his reader through paragraph twelve:

The principle which you appear to regard as violated by the transaction in question, may be stated as follows:—*Every man has a natural and inalienable right to himself.* The inference from this is, '*that man cannot hold property in man*'—*and as man cannot hold property in man, neither can Hugh Auld nor the United States have any right of property in me—and having no right of property in me, they have no right to sell me—and having no right to sell me, no one has a right to buy me.* I think I have now stated the principle, and the inference from the principle, distinctly and fairly. Now, the question upon which the whole controversy turns is, simply, this: does the transaction, which you condemn, really violate this principle? I own that, to a superficial observer, it would seem to do so. But I think I am prepared to show, that, so far from being a violation of that principle, it is truly a noble vindication of it. Before going further, let me state here, briefly, what sort of a purchase would have been a violation of this principle, which, in common with yourself, I reverence and am anxious to preserve inviolate.

1st. It would have been a violation of that principle, had those who purchased me done so, *to make me a slave, instead of a freeman.*

And,

2ndly. It would have been a violation of that principle, had those who purchased me done so with a view to compensate the slaveholder, for what he and they regarded as his rightful property.

In *paragraph thirteen*, Douglass employs *the descriptive mode* to convey a sense of the attitudes of those who interceded on his behalf. This section is supported by details presented by the use of *the narrative mode*. Toward the end of the paragraph he uses *the descriptive mode* to convey a sense of the attitudes of those who misunderstand the motives of his intercessors:

In neither of these ways was my purchase effected. My liberation was, in their estimation, of more value than £150; the happiness and repose of my family were, in their judgment, more than paltry gold. The £150 was paid to the remorseless plunderer, not because he had any just claim to it, but to induce him to give up his legal claim to something which they deemed of more value than money. It was not to compensate the slaveholder, but to release me from his power; not to establish my *natural right* to freedom, but to release me from all legal liabilities to slavery. And all this, you and I, and the slaveholders, and all who know anything of the transaction, very well understand. The very letter to Hugh Auld, proposing terms of purchase, informed him that those who gave, *denied his right to it.* The error of those, who condemn this transaction, consists in their confounding the crime of buying men *into slavery,* with the meritorious act of buying men out of slavery, and the purchase of legal freedom with abstract right and natural freedom. They say, 'If you *buy*, you recognize the right to sell. If you receive, you recognize the right of the giver to give.' And this has a show of truth, as well as of logic. But a few plain cases will show its entire fallacy.

Moving from paragraph thirteen to fourteen, Douglass makes a transition to another stage of analysis and proceeds to lay out and elaborate upon the next stage:

There is now, in this country, a heavy duty on corn. The government of this country has imposed it; and though I regard it a most unjust and wicked imposition, no man of common sense will charge me with endorsing or recognizing the right of this government to impose this duty, simply because, to prevent myself and family from starving, I buy and eat this corn.

Paragraph fifteen proceeds mainly through Douglass' use of *the narrative mode*. He uses a hypothetical case in order to make another point in his argument:

Take another case:—I have had dealings with a man. I have owed him one hundred dollars, and have paid it; I have lost the receipt. He comes upon me the second time for the money. I know, and he knows, he has no right to it; but he is a villain, and has me in his power. The law is with him, and against me. I must pay or be dragged to jail. I choose to pay the bill a second time. To say I sanctioned his right to rob me, because I preferred to pay rather than go to jail, is to utter an absurdity, to which no sane man would give heed. And yet the principle of action, in each of these cases, is the same. The man might indeed say, the claim is unjust—and declare, I will rot in jail, before I will pay it. But this would not, certainly, be demanded by any principle of truth, justice, or humanity; and however much we might be disposed to respect his daring, but little deference could be paid to his wisdom. The fact is, we act upon this principle every day of our lives, and we have an undoubted right to do so. When I came to this country from the United States, I came in the *second* cabin. And why? Not because my natural right to come in the *first* cabin was not as good as that of any other man, but because a wicked and cruel prejudice decided, that the second cabin was the place for me. By coming over in the second, did I sanction or justify this wicked proscription? Not at all. It was the best I could do. I acted from necessity.

Paragraph sixteen moves from the use of *expository mode* to the *descriptive mode;* then it moves to the *narrative mode* and back to the *expository:*

One other case, and I have done with this view of the subject. I think you will agree with me, that the case I am now about to put is pertinent, though you may not readily pardon me for making yourself the agent of my illustration. The case respects the passport system on the Continent of Europe. That system you utterly condemn. You look upon it as an unjust and wicked interference, a bold and infamous violation of the sacred right of locomotion. You hold, (and so do I,) that the image of our common God ought to be a passport all over the habitable world. But bloody and tyrannical governments have ordained otherwise; they usurp authority over you, and decide for you, on what conditions you shall travel. They say, you shall have a passport, or you shall be put in prison. Now, the question is, have they a right to prescribe any such terms? and do you, by complying with these terms, sanction their interference? I think you will answer, no; submission to injustice, and sanction of injustice, are different things; and he is a poor reasoner who confounds the two, and makes them one and the same thing. Now, then, for the parallel, and the application of the passport system to my own case.

In *paragraph seventeen*, Douglass uses *the descriptive and narrative modes* to relate H. C. Wright's having been once caught in a situation similar to his own:

I wish to go to the United States. I have a natural right to go there, and be free. My natural right is as good as that of Hugh Auld, or James K. Polk; but that plundering government says, I shall not return to the United States in safety—it says, I must allow Hugh Auld to rob me, or my friends, of £150, or be hurled into the infernal jaws of slavery. I must have a 'bit of paper, signed and sealed,' or my liberty must be taken from me, and I must be torn from my family and friends. The government of Austria said to you, 'Dare to come upon my soil, without a passport, declaring you to be an American citizen, (which you say you are not,) you shall at once be arrested, and thrown into prison.' What said you to that Government? Did you say that the threat was a villanous one, and an infamous invasion of your right of locomotion? Did you say, 'I will come upon your soil; I will go where I please! I dare and defy your government!' Did you say, 'I will spurn your passports; I would not stain my hand, and degrade myself, by touching your miserable parchment. You have no right to give it, and I have no right to take it. I trample your laws, and will put your constitutions under my feet! I will not recognize them!' Was this your course? No! dear friend, it was not. Your practice was wiser than your theory. You took the passport, submitted to be examined while travelling, and availed yourself of all the advantages of your 'passport'—or, in other words, escaped all the evils which you ought to have done, without it, and would have done,

66

but for the tyrannical usurpation in Europe.

In *paragraph eighteen,* Douglass begins to conclude by summary, using *exposition* as his primary mode:

I will not dwell longer upon this view of the subject; and I dismiss it, feeling quite satisfied of the entire correctness of the reasoning, and the principle attempted to be maintained. As to the expediency of the measures, different opinions may well prevail; but in regard to the principle, I feel it difficult to conceive of two opinions. I am free to say, that, had I possessed one hundred and fifty pounds, I would have seen Hugh Auld *kicking,* before I would have given it to him. I would have waited till the emergency came, and only given up the money when nothing else would do. But my friends thought it best to provide against the contingency; they acted on their own responsibility, and I am not disturbed about the result. But, having acted on a true principle, I *do not feel free to disavow their proceedings.*

The whole of *paragraph nineteen* is a formal conclusion of the argument. Douglass uses *expository* reiteration here as well as a final *descriptive* labelling of the American republic as the culprit fostering his condition:

In conclusion, let me say, I anticipate no such change in my position as you predict. I shall be Frederick Douglass still, and once a slave still. I shall neither be made to forget nor cease to feel the wrongs of my enslaved fellow-countrymen. My knowledge of slavery will be the same, and my hatred of it will be the same. By the way, I have never made my own person and suffering the theme of public discourse, but have always based my appeal upon the wrongs of the three millions now in chains; and these shall still be the burthen of my speeches. You intimate that I may reject the papers, and allow them to remain in the hands of those friends who have effected the purchase, and thus avail myself of the security afforded by them, without sharing any part of the responsibility of the transaction. My objection to this is one of honor. I do not think it would be very honorable on my part, to remain silent during the whole transaction, and giving it more than my silent approval; and then, when the thing is completed, and I am safe, attempt to play the *hero*, by throwing off all responsibility in the matter. It might be

67

said, and said with great propriety, 'Mr. Douglass, your indignation is very good, and has but one fault, and that is, *it comes too late!*' It would be a show of bravery when the danger is over. From every view I have been able to take of the subject, I am persuaded to receive the papers, if presented,—not, however, as a proof of my right to be free, for *that is self-evident,* but as a proof that my friends have been legally robbed of £150, in order to secure that which is the birth-right of every man. And I will hold up those papers before the world, in proof of the plundering character of the American government. It shall be the brand of infamy, stamping the nation, in whose name the deed was done, as a great aggregation of hypocrites, thieves and liars,—and their condemnation is just. They declare that all men are created equal, and have a natural and inalienable right to liberty, while they rob me of £150, as a condition of my enjoying this natural and inalienable right. It will be their condemnation, in their own hand-writing, and may be held up to the world as a means of humbling that haughty republic into repentance.

Douglass concludes the argumentative letter to H. C. Wright with some *exposition,* some *description,* and some hypothetical *narration:*

I agree with you, that the contest which I have to wage is against the government of the United States. But the representative of that government is the slaveholder, *Thomas Auld.* He is commander-in-chief of the army and navy. The whole civil and naval force of the nation are at his disposal. He may command all these to his assistance, and bring them all to bear upon me, until I am made entirely subject to his will, or submit to be robbed myself, or allow my friends to be robbed, of seven hundred and fifty dollars. And rather than be subject to his will, I have submitted to be robbed, or allowed my friends to be robbed, of the seven hundred and fifty dollars.

Sincerely yours,

FREDERICK DOUGLASS

INDEX

Active engagement, 12
Analysis, 17
Argumentation, 28-29, 58-68
Arrangement of parts, 14
Authority, 11, 15
Bibliography, 40, 42-43
Body of essay, 20
Book review essay, 51-55
Boundaries, 14
Brainstorming, 19, 20
Character, 17
Citations, 37-50
Clarity, 12, 14, 16, 17, 18, 19, 23
Colon, 35-36
Comma, 31-34
Comparison-contrast techniques, 29-30
Conclusions, 12, 20
Coherence, 14, 16, 19
Confidence, 12-13, 17, 21, 52
Consciousness, 16, 20

Control, 12, 18, 22
Credibility, 11, 15
Critical thinking, 16
Criticism, 13, 57
Defending your point, 13, 20
Demonstration, 14, 15
Description, 27, 29
Development, 13, 20
Diction, 24
Discernment, 12
Discipline, 15
Discourse, modes of, 26-29, 58-68
Discrimination, 15
Discussion, 17
Documentation, 37-50
Drafting, 19, 23
Effective writing, 12, 14, 16, 17, 18, 23
Endnotes, 40, 49
Engagement with writing, 12, 13
Essay, definition, 25
Essays, categories, 26
Evaluation of the writer, 12
Examining your subject, 14, 15, 17
Exposition, 27, 29
Fluency, 18, 21
Focus, 13, 14, 18, 20-21
Footnotes, 40
Fundamental steps of writing, 9
Gesture, 16
Good thinking, 15, 16
Good writer, 11, 12, 13, 15, 17, 18
Grammar, 11, 24
Ideas, 16, 17, 20

Identity of the writer, 12, 18
Image, 17
Inner growth, 12
Internal notes, 40, 43-44
Interpretation, 12, 17, 22
Intonation, 16
Introductions, 12, 19, 20, 21
Investigation, 14
Language, 11, 12, 13
Logic, 15
Narration, 26-27, 29
Notetaking, 20, 22
Order, 19
Organization, 13, 15, 17, 18, 19, 20, 21-22, 23
Outlining, 20
Paragraph, definition, 25
Parenthetical notes, 43-45
Passing the reader's test, 14, 15, 17
Plagiarism, 38-39
Planning, 13, 14
Pitch, 16
Point-of-view, 13, 17, 21
Precision, 13
Problems with writing, 11
Progression of thought, 13
Proof, 14
Punctuation, 15, 24, 31-36
Purpose, 14
Reading techniques, 17, 18, 22
Reference citations, 37-42
Research papers, 20
Responding to your subject, 14, 15
Restricting the subject, 14

Re-writing, 18, 19, 22
Rhythm, 18, 21
Scrutinizing, 23
Self-concept, 12, 18
Self defeat, 14
Self-scrutiny, 15, 18
Semi-colon, 34-35
Sentence definition, 24
Sentence structure, 18
Slang, 16
Standards, 15, 17
Starting, 19, 20
Strengths, 19, 57
Style, 16, 18
Style manuals for research papers, 41-42
Subject matter, 12, 14, 15, 16, 17, 18
Support, 14, 15
Syntax, 24
Theme, 17
Thesis statement, 14, 21
Thoroughness, 13, 15
Thoughts, 11, 14, 15, 16, 17, 18, 19
Time, 19, 20, 23
Title, 14
Topic, 15
Trust of the writer, 13
Unity, 19
Vocabulary, 16
Weaknesses, 19, 57
Writer's block, 22
Writing process, 12, 17
Writing skills, 17, 19

Erskine Peters holds a Ph.D. in English from Princeton University. He is a graduate of Paine College and has also studied at Yale University and Oberlin College.

Dr. Peters is currently Professor of English at the University of Notre Dame. Prior to that he was Associate Professor of Afro-American Studies at the University of California, Berkeley.

Dr. Peters is also the author of *William Faulkner: The Yoknapatawpha World and Black Being* (1983), and *African Openings to the Tree of Life* (1984), originally published by Norwood Editions, Darby, Pennsylvania and now available from Regent Press.

The author and publisher would be grateful to have comments and suggestions from the users of this book.

- NOTES -